NOCTURNES OF THE BROTHEL OF RUIN

Also by Patrick Donnelly
 The Charge

Translations with Stephen D. Miller
 *The Wind from Vulture Peak: The Buddhification of Japanese
 Waka in the Heian Period*

NOCTURNES OF THE BROTHEL OF RUIN

PATRICK DONNELLY

including translations from the Japanese
with Stephen D. Miller

FOUR WAY BOOKS

TRIBECA

Please direct all inquiries to:
Editorial Office
Four Way Books
POB 535, Village Station
New York, NY 10014
www.fourwaybooks.com

Library of Congress Cataloging-in-Publication Data

Donnelly, Patrick, 1956-
 Nocturnes of the brothel of ruin : poems / by Patrick Donnelly including translations
from the Japanese with Stephen D. Miller.
     p. cm.
Includes bibliographical references.
ISBN 978-1-935536-21-5 (pbk. : alk. paper)
I. Miller, Stephen D., 1949- II. Title.
PS3604.O5634N63 2012
811'.6--dc23

                          2011027990

This book is manufactured in the United States of America
and printed on acid-free paper.

Four Way Books is a not-for-profit literary press. We are grateful for the assistance
we receive from individual donors, public arts agencies, and private foundations.

This publication is made possible with public funds
from the New York State Council on the Arts, a state agency.

Distributed by University Press of New England
One Court Street, Lebanon, NH 03766

[clmp] We are a proud member
of the Council of Literary Magazines and Presses.

Cover Art: *A Turkish Cypriot receives a back-cracking massage at Korkut Baths,*
National Geographic. Used with permission.

TABLE OF CONTENTS

II

III

for Stephen

kimi narade
tare ni ka misen
ume no hana
iro o mo ka o mo
shiru hito zo shiru

and

for my mother and father

I give him songs, he gives me length of days.

WHEN IN THE UTERINE EMPYREAN THEY TOLD ME

When in the uterine empyrean they told me

of love, they named it a *sickness, fever, impediment
to enlightenment.* Some swore it could make you wail
over hills of hell in a long black veil, defenestrate

yourself in a Second Empire gown, or stand
wringing-wet at the intersection with a cup and a sign
reading COMFORT ME WITH APPLES.

There were a few, humiliated and exalted, who rose
like comets in yellowy tiers, to sing in Provençal
of the Name, the Name, the same longing Name.

But others warned that *whom He loves, He corrects,*
of "friendship with benefits," balcony scenes, mad scenes
in all-white restaurants, of the turned back in bed.

But when they said I could remain behind
if I chose, like an unlit lamp,
sounding my brass and tinkling my cymbal,

I didn't think, I seized
the bloody flag of my attachments
and tore down the tunnel of what I couldn't know

was my millionth birth.

I

THE GATE TO EVERYWHERE

yo o sukuu

the world is saved

because no one can shut
the gate to everywhere: O who

will not enter?

from the Japanese of Former Major Counsellor Kintō

BEFORE THE FALL

I flew and tore my pants at the knee,
but before that trip I was happy,
thought the way was clear.
Later I washed my little wound
at a sink, paid for needle and thread
at the newsstand with a hand that shook.
                              The shock
not from bleeding, but from being caught
not knowing I'd have to kneel
on stones in front of strangers.

ON THE LUNGS, THE LIVER, AND THE BLOOD

A hard rain came that broke
the afternoon heat, then at dusk upstream
of Togetsukyo Bridge a man with a rake
began to clear the weir of what
an old poem calls *mikuzu:*
oddments, litter, confusion, a boot, all a metaphor
in the poem for the speaker, who
is bound to die. The rain trapped
two boys smoking on benches
in an open hut, with a woman
who checked her phone as one might gaze
at one's own face in a mirror, and an old man
whose dog barked at thunder, river, smoke,
umbrellas crossing the bridge,
cafés, sweetshops, and the intersection
where thin brown rickshaw boys
huddled under katsura leaves.
Just below where the man tilled his spot
but out of reach, a sad anomaly evolved
that forced the same trash to circle
with no hope of escape, unless someday Amida really
does arrive from the West with his net.
The river rose until the defile
where the man stood roared with a brown foam.
Every time the flume clogged, the man
cleared it. Without hope,
therefore strangely moving. A moon

rose and offered to rake
clouds away from the mountain,
but lit his service little, who stood
in sweat and mizzle to open
one place where
the river needed to flow.

LINK

Trying to talk himself
        out of a tremor, he argued
                it's not just this interview
decides the outcome of many years:
        every gesture triggers
                a cascade of ghost-futures, reels
Mars and Venus around
        the roulette of their mansions.
                So don't sweat any particular node,
look to the protection of the whole,
        a pattern that seen
                from a distance seems to hold,
has held. Remember how, in the city, September
        those years ago, midnight began
                the day you'd turn forty-seven?
You didn't know it, but
        if you clicked that pulsing link,
                if you followed where it led,
you'd marry
        in the Commonwealth.
                If not, you'd live
every single year
        and die alone.

ALL IN BLACK

my love went stretching
      up to the grip-
strap, tensing, releasing
        perfume like a cathedral.

Imagined love only, in those days,
      whose mouth
hung sullen and whose wrists perfect.

He refused to look
            at me, cracking
the spine of his book.

ON LEARNING THAT THE PHONE IN A HOUSE WHERE HE LIVED THIRTY YEARS AGO IS STILL IN HIS NAME

If I could call him to the phone
who lived there then,
maybe interrupting those lovemakings
that almost broke the green chair
(with, among others, the pianist
whose slender hands had Mozart in them,
and went cold as young),

it would only be to warn: go ahead,
move to the city again, let yourself
charge down the same strait
between clashing rocks, between those
burning voids and frozen viral graves.

Because, Patrick—
if you try to hunger or love more carefully
no one from the future will breathe your name,

and you will still die—

stupid, hungry, without
having burned the dross off your blood.

CONSERVATIVE

Once I loved a guy who foresaw not disaster
              but glory crowning
              every commencement.
The morning he began a screenplay,
              in his peripheral vision
              a starlet handed him
a statuette. When he died at thirty-five, a paralegal,
              to me his dreams
              seemed blasted, but I believe
he was a happy man.
                    Me, I expect catastrophe,
              so I police my levees,
              disconnect delicate devices
at first threat of thunder. This blue and white bowl
              I paid to repair
              after a move. In its hollow
two boys in smocks wind cows and sheep
              to market
              down a cottage lane.
A lamb strays into the gilliflowers, unnoticed
              by the careless
              younger boy,
who puts all his weight on one foot, circles his arms
              over his head and looks
              out of the bowl at the world.
The older brother turns back, half-listening
              to his mother's last few words,
              herself half-hidden

under a briar hung from the reedy eaves.
                    In the deciduous distance,
                    roofs and spires
of a cathedral town can just be glimpsed,
                    maybe the Salisbury
                    I circled slowly
the sunny September of a year I was sick.
                    On the western curve,
                    a border collie lowers its head
in that way of theirs, herding some sound
                    or smell
                    out of a cave.
                                        A wordless man
smelling of benzine, who studied crockery repair
                    forty years,
                    and his father before him,
made the bowl whole. One of identical three,
                    it can't bear
                    heat, cold, wet,
or hold anything it used to hold. But to the eye
                    it's perfect,
                    so I marked
the bottom with a thick black X.

PRAYER FOR IMMUNITY IN GRAND ARMY PLAZA

At a quarter to dusk
a moon froze in the groin of an elm,
horses on the arch dragged their bronze wagon
through Brooklyn toward another war.

When I was young in the desert they warned
never walk *arroyos* when it rains,
water can crash down those gullies
in minutes, from a hundred miles away.

This street I love
could come apart that fast,
like bread in water.

But my love
is alive in a little town to the west,
where there's two more hours of sun,
where there's still time.

Does everyone in danger pray
the same stupid prayer?—
strike the next house, the neighbors
who had their love all along.

I found my life so late—
leave me a little time
to love his grayblue eyes forgiving
what is unworthy in mine.

IN GLUCK'S HAPPY ENDING

the gods relent, the lovers reunite.

Cue the key of D major, the ballet of shepherds
and shepherdesses, the tender crowns of daylilies—

for those who can't bear
the pure Greek truth:

no kind of singing can bring back the dead.

THREAT

He thumbs a corner of Verlaine,
      plucks those pages like a dulcimer,
even when the train lurches
      not looking up
but pawing at the air for a handhold,
      and my God! what a head—
stamped from some stuff lustrous
      as the first coin from the first mint,
fresh and firm—as my love and I can't be,
      bloom long rubbed off the plums,
our skin all mottled and creased,
      bellies bloated with worry—
and the worst is, somehow
      around this boy too
floats a threat,
      young as he is, when he exhales
a scent of smoke and roses,
      smoking roses, roses on fire,
like a flame surrounding a flame—

      but as I disembark I swear

by the million times I've broken
    my alabaster urn
over the beautiful temples of strangers

    I won't look back,

      and I don't.

SENT TO THE MOUNTAIN TEMPLE WHERE I HEARD
JITSUHAN SHŌNIN HAD SECLUDED HIMSELF

kokoro ni wa

how you must loathe
           the world
                to flee it—
but O—
      isn't the world
           still sad
there—
    here—
        everywhere?

from the Japanese of Jōgon Hōshi

CRYING THE DIVINE NAME IN ARABIC ON HIGHWAY 80

Bismillah leaning away from the demon hauling gas
Bismillah seducing the governor over seventy-seven miles per hour

Bismillah threading every narrow gap, with every frail thing we hope
crossing high over the Susquehanna bolting through her gorge,
      flooded and muddy

Bismillah after a longed-for piss, then again to wash my hands; *Bismillah*
sweetening my speech, too ironic, certain, barking and large for our little cab

In That Name,
In That subtly vibrating, taken-for-granted-and-in-vain Name

lifting our fat bag every night from the truck,
lifting spoons of soup to our fond, humid mouths

Bismillah that ever we met; *Bismillah* on tiptoe of duty and dread
at the door of your mother's slow succumbing

Bismillah Who slipped the world dripping and perfect onto its mighty hinge
Bismillah Who put me delicate in my mother's pocket

Alhumdulillah when we accomplish
as we sleep the years-sought hush of the other and the other's breath

Bismillah for dangers I expect,
Bismillah for dangers I dream not of

for dumb creatures, crossing safely or not
(oh poor meat, poor pelt, *Bismillah*)

one moment after the crack-up that tears me
however it must out of *us*

though not now, not soon, not crash
anywhere along here in the wet ditch, blown and broken

apart from this rough praise, God willing *Bismillah*
and not *shit* the final cry I make

PARABLE OF THE CONJURED CITY

michi toomi

go back? halfway there?

because the road is long?

(though if I imagine
there's a place I might
rest for a moment

it does cheer me)

from the Japanese of Mother of Yasusuke no Ō

PARADISE ON BLACK ICE

Heaven hunts round for those that find itself below, and then it snatches.
  —*Emily Dickinson*

I wind
the sheet of elegy

while he's still alive, I can't help it,
I follow his breath while he sleeps,

greet each coming and going,
with an *Ave*.
     (Because of how
the quick
become the dead.)

But right now he's showering
with a gospel choir, radio

half on and half off that station.
And today's heaven is half hell,

half whole, half hurt,
hunting every naked thing

with the same harsh delight.

THICK

His first name,
        oddly girlish,

is all I recall of him
        now, and how

he unbuckled the thick
        braid of his belt

as he reclined, and let me
        attend to all the rest.

NOCTURNES OF THE BROTHEL OF RUIN

First Lesson: Aleph

Never Christmas there. Never Thanksgiving:
always the same day and no day,
the same twilight, the same pounding
from overhead, and no one had a name.
If you asked a man for a name, he'd pause
and whatever name he said
would not be his real name, the number
he gave not his real number. If later
you called, a phone would ring and ring
somewhere in the wrong dark.

Second Lesson: Beth

. . . he needed ten minutes
with my cock, a gift I'd given him
a dozen times for free. And I needed
money, so that one time I required it.
The exchange seemed fair, at first.
But the way he threw the money
on the narrow bed, saying "for you, anytime,"
the way my love which began as religion
ended as commerce . . .

Third Lesson: Ghimel

His heart
gabbled endearments,
secret even from himself:
"Come," it cried,
"desperado, camerado, my mikado,
O root, O key, O king," etc., eventually referencing
all the lovely antiphons of advent.

Fourth Lesson: Daleth

Handsome lean surfer dude
played with my ass:
"We're not going far that way.
There's a brick wall, so to speak."
Wiped my shit on my thigh.

Fifth Lesson: He

John, you said your name was,
and offered your hand to be shook,
which was absurd, there.
It was like kissing a little deer
to stroke the fine hair
at the back of your neck, to run
my hand over your belly

which was both soft and hard.
I moved carefully to cup your ear
in my mouth and breathe,
hoping you might let me pretend
we were in love. But after a moment
you said, "Let's take a break,"
which, in the language of that place
meant: *I'm through,*
there are others . . .

Sixth Lesson: Vav

Ten cops sprinted up the stairs
through the line of waiting men: a call
to save a customer who wouldn't wake up,
who never woke up again.

Seventh and Last Lesson: Zain

The Prophet Jesus, peace be upon him,
rapped gently at the door of the cubicle.

"Are you about ready to go?" he asked.

"I'm not sure . . ."
               The man pulled a towel
over himself as the Prophet sat and lit

a cigarette, Turkish, with a little sugar
at the tip, the burning nub the brightest thing
in the room as it passed between them.
The Prophet smoked with obvious enjoyment,
and when he exhaled over the man,
he renovated him
from the head down
on seven interior levels.

"I was looking for you everywhere,"
the man said, "I gave up."
"I know," the Prophet answered,
"would you like to get some breakfast?"

(Or maybe what he said was, "break your fast.")

Outside, as always, a row of ten yellow taxis
waited, drivers ready to ferry anyone
who wanted to go to the black cube
at the center of the universe.
In the cab the man made a pillow
of the Prophet's thigh, and lost
what tears he had been holding.

PANTOUM OF THE BROTHEL OF RUIN

Some things you see remain mysterious for years.
It happened at the baths in the small hours.
I swear to God it's true, though I dislike that term.
There were three doors to the anteroom.

It happened at the baths in the small hours.
You waited in line until you had paid.
There were three doors to the anteroom.
There was no conversation in line, but you could look.

You waited in line until you had paid.
You tended to think about what you hoped would happen inside.
There was no conversation in line, but you could look.
The wait could be long. I always brought a book.

You tended to think about what you hoped would happen inside.
The door behind us led down the stairs to the street.
There was no conversation in line, but you could look.
The doors on either side of where you paid were locked.

The door behind us led down the stairs to the street.
After you paid, the clerk buzzed open the door on the right.
The doors on either side of where you paid were locked.
The door on the right led in to the twilit maze.

After you paid, the clerk buzzed open the door on the right.
Each leaving man pushed out of the door on the left.
The door on the right led in to the twilit maze.
The door on the left led out of the twilit maze.

Each leaving man pushed out of the door on the left.
After four hours you had to pay again, or leave.
The door on the left led out of the twilit maze.
You left with high color, wet hair, sometimes soft eyes.

After four hours you had to pay again, or leave.
On Friday night the line snaked halfway down to the street.
You left with high color, wet hair, sometimes soft eyes.
Out of nowhere, a young Hasidic Jew materialized.

On Friday night the line snaked halfway down to the street.
His face was pale and his beard cut short.
Out of nowhere, a young Hasidic Jew materialized.
In a black satin coat and a high beaver hat.

His face was pale and his beard cut short.
He dashed in the "out" door, as an astonished guy came through.
In a black satin coat and a high beaver hat.
I remember his entrance as more horizontal than vertical.

He dashed in the "out" door, as an astonished guy came through.
White fringes and spaniel ringlets flying behind.
I remember his entrance as more horizontal than vertical.
Like Elizabeth Barrett Browning in a windtunnel.

White fringes and spaniel ringlets flying behind.
Because he hadn't paid to enter, he would have had no key.
Like Elizabeth Barrett Browning in a windtunnel.
He would have had no place to go, no room of his own.

Because he hadn't paid to enter, he would have had no key.
Did he arrive in one passionate lunge from the street?
He would have had no place to go, no room of his own.
Or had he watched for a chance, from some hidden, closer place?

Did he arrive in one passionate lunge from the street?
He had to go in the "out" door, I long ago decided.
But had he watched for a chance from some hidden, closer place?
Because the Pentateuch licked the door the rest of us took with flame,

he had to go in the "out" door, I long ago decided.
I swear to God it's true, though I dislike that term.
O, had he watched for a chance from some hidden, closer place?
Some things you see remain mysterious for years.

yo no naka ni

    if there were in the world
        no jeweled chariot
            drawn by a lovely white ox

           what would coax us out
      of the burning house

    of our mind?

from an anonymous Japanese poem

MY DOCTOR USED TO PRAISE MY EARS,

how clean, how faultless, I remember
     as I probe with a swab,

and my skin flushes proud to remember,
     as though I were different from the others

who didn't take care, who threw away
     their ears and their lives, some so past caring

they shuffled through his surgery
     in shackles from the local jail,

guards watching while they clambered
     naked into the light of his cold tables.

As though *daintiness* could save me.
     As though he could,
               who disappeared
his own handsome self,
     after a month of sweats and shakes.

CORPSE FLOWER

Amorphophallus titanum

If that squeamish virgin Artemis in the *Hippolytus* of Euripides was right—
    even to look on death makes you unclean,

if the people were right who hauled Taguchi Shigeyuki nine hundred
    years ago out of their house on a sliding door
so he wouldn't die inside, if they were right to believe death pollutes a house,

if the singing teacher of my twenties last night was right when she scolded
    me *at fifty-one you are too young to think of death so much,*

even so, soil me, roll me in the funk of it.

No other flower blooms as large. Huge.

II

the debt
    I owe the breasts
        my mother in tender mercy gave—

        to one hundred stones
    add eighty—

I repay today

from the Japanese of Gyōki

INVOCATION

Little fishes:

let the fires I hang at night
in iron cages over your waters call
you to the verge, high
in your world as you are allowed to go,

and then higher.

Sweetfish, blonde with lack
of light, smelling of melon
and cucumber milk.

Come to my cressets, gather
and assume a shape. Come
up to the painful air
and gasp
        again as you did
in life.
       Let yourself be caught,
let me catch you with the beak
of my pen, as the cormorant
catches, not to swallow,
but to spit, cough up, feed
the hungry. Let

the dead school that was my mother

live.

MY MOTHER TRIES TO QUIT

My mother is an animal of smoke.
I'll do better now, her message says,
I'm not strong but
I'll be better now.

My mother's house is sixty years of smoke,
the box she sent exhaled what she inhaled,
the book in the box exhaled her breath,
the poems in the book exhaled her breath,
the poems she wasn't strong enough to speak aloud
she sent to me, still smoking.

Finally, she said, *I could hold it in my hand,*
but couldn't inhale.

The book was Yeats:

I put him in the window to breathe.

RECEIVED WISDOM

I thought my mother gave me words,
because she loved and brandished words
between the smoker's ash of her laughs
and her narrative sighs, audible
from the back of the house like those
of any really good tragedienne.

So when the time came, it was her
interesting chromosomes I thanked
in those places acknowledgements
are made,
           and never mentioned the father
whose words to me seemed dull
and desolate.

Not until I learned
how the world is built between its poles
did I understand he also helped fund
that cursive fountain in me:

by laying the Y of his ice

next to her X of fire.

MY STEPMOTHER FEEDS THE BIRDS OF GETHSEMANE

To she who tried to mother me
in the absence of my mother:

who married a gentle man after my father:

who had a way of pushing fallen hair
away from her dark eyes as though
she suffered her own face:

who did not denounce
the wandering preacher for an old crime,
but repeated the Our Father at home
until he had packed his tent and gone:

who begged my father all of one night
to retrieve me from a man
with whom he had left me:

whose frightened question the next morning I did not answer:

who feeds her birds food she has chewed
from her own mouth:

whose voice when she answers the phone
is never as though she imagines any good of it:

whose question I am ready to answer,
if she will ask me again:

to take away this cup
of tears and fire and gall.

MUDRA

Who
gives you authority to speak? Who
died and crowned your head? Where
in hell do you get off?,
asked an undermining spirit named Mara
one day as I sat to write, in a hoarse baritone
just like my mother's at the end, when
from her curtained bed she spat *by now*
I shouldn't be surprised at your pompous side,
how you puff out your chest when you talk—

only by luck not her last words.

Who gives me right?

No teacher, not anymore;
not my father, who spoke few words,
none of the judges who choose
whose words to set in type,
and nobody's notion of a god.

But from long practice
noticing what I was told not to notice,
practice touching my forehead
to the bellies of forbidden strangers in the dark,
practice extending sympathetic embassies toward everything
low and dangerous in myself,

I'm able to point at last, oh happy fault,
at the germ of my authority—
the chafe that bled a pearl—

in *you*, mother,

as I forgive the carbon
of your shadow in myself, my dear
and mortal adversary.

CALLED BACK

Nobody knows me here anymore.

I'm not the boy back from Iraq
the airport crowd was waiting for
with signs and balloons at the bottom of the escalator,

not the trucker the motel looked to greet
with thin towels, blankets full of burns,
red-letter Bibles like valentines
the Gideons keep sending
to the tempted, weary, convicted-of-doubt,

not the kind of son
who might have spent these last months
adjusting her fan, telling nurses where she hurt,
agreeing or at least listening
when she swore she called and called
and no one ever came.

Therefore though I spent a night
studying, testing, whispering,
and towards dawn just plain bawling it,

that Word

left for me to find
in the drawer by the bed, in the shallow, narrow drawer
smelling of pine—

could not abide with me.

WING-BACKED PRAYER

Let yourself go, let your neck
relax and your jaw go slack.
Be cheerful, willing to be comforted.
Relax pride, relax even the locks
that hold back everything unclean.
Leave us your checks, your silver forks,
try to believe we'll do for you
as well or better what
you used to do for yourself.

She phoned to say it *scared the shit* out of her
she couldn't sit up or remember.

Nothing suggests I'll die easier
or more kind.

If the air around us were still,
it might be warm as wool.
But the air is not still, nothing
ever will hold still.

Now that she's coughed up
her last curse, my counsels
neither heard nor unheard:

You

who keep Your counsels close

help me lift a word
from my lap to my lips,

help me imagine
vanity might die
some hour
before I do.

tsune yori mo

it hurts
     that what I mistook
          for today's spring mist

          is just the smoke of wood
     that has been
consumed by the fire

from the Japanese of Former Preceptor Keisen

OXYGEN CATASTROPHE

Mon vieux, you say cremation,
you can't help feeling, is a gesture
ungrateful to the body
and the giver of the body.

But I (who have for years at a time
lived, reclined, frolicked, pranked, played the fool
in low, unworthy rooms, far too full
of gratefulness, of a kind, for my body) wonder:

do you mean the same dear giver
of the sweet sweet air
that is already burning
your body, mine, our memory, my memory of

a black and white collie in the spring,
the spring,
the seraphim,
these letters,

everything?

CRADLE-SONG

When I signed for her ashes

I received her, as once
        she received me
into her lyric hold
        and let me ride anchor there,
smaller than the letter *alif.*

They gave her into my hands,
        seven pounds, two ounces,
as once they had given
        me into her hands.

I set her on the hearth shrine,
        as she set me once a place at her table,
among her other needy charities.

After nine months I scattered her
        back to that cold, delphine Atlantic of hers,
to tidal squalls that rip
        and sigh their salt across the rocks,

as once she let me fall

unready
        onto this world's
gasping, shouting, love-stained shore.

THE MOTHER'S ASHES REPLY

when he put—when that man put my
        ashes in the water,

for the space of four
        green waves

I held together as a knot of
        milk

then a fifth thing of—water?—broke
        open my last

seals and—

                delivered

        me to be

                        no body

        and no body's

                        mama

TO HER TEACHER

kuraki yori

the path I had to take
led from dark
to darker—

O moon

on your mountain edge
shine across
the vast emptiness

from the Japanese of Izumi Shikibu

HOMELAND

after Eichendorff

A flash of red told me, from that direction,
some smoke from the south, from the past,
the west, from her house, her town, where
I grew up, told me *mother is dead a little while* . . .

Now nobody knows me there anymore.

How soon? How soon will the time come
when I pull to the west, when I lean,
too, into the dirt and rest, and over me
rushes the leaves' sweet secret loneliness,

and nobody knows me here anymore—

ON THE ESSENCE OF THE *WELLING UP OUT OF THE EARTH* CHAPTER

tarachine wa

the mother's hair
        is black but

the child's eyebrows
        have turned white—

how is it possible?

from the Japanese of Gon no Sōjō Yōen

SKYLIGHT

blue eye from which my eye got born—

    she, who saw
                with a fine eye once—

remember how she closed

    with duct tape and the bottom of a box

that opening the architect designed

    for her last roof?
                which let in light and

trouble, a long waste of sky

WHEN THE EMPEROR'S PLANS FOR A CELEBRATION IN HIS MOTHER'S HONOR WERE CUT SHORT BY HER DEATH

itsu shika to

      the tender
    shoots of spring
I picked today—

I wanted to hurry them
  to you for
      your journey

from the Japanese of Gyosei, the Tenryaku Emperor

THE SISTER'S COMPLAINT WAS

he was
two thousand three hundred ninety-one

miles away every 3 AM
their mother called from across town:

her breath, her cough, her voice,
I was so tired, I just wanted to sleep.

Will you send me pictures
of her when she was young, of myself

as a child?
I've been asking and asking, but you

never send.
Her bills, her shrink, her date of birth.

At least
you have the memory, beautiful I guess,

of her cloud of ash
in the green water, or however you put it.

But what I have is,
when I open the cupboard where I keep

a few of her things,

I smell smoke.

III

SENT TO ISE NO TAYŪ ON THE FIFTEENTH OF THE SECOND MONTH IN THE MIDDLE OF THE NIGHT

ikanareba

why
          instead of shining
                    to the end

                    did the moon of evening
          go inside the veil
during the night's small hours?

from the Japanese of Priest Keihan

AN ANSWER

yo o terasu

during the night's small hours
    the moon
        that shone over the world

        has hidden—will everyone
    have been lost
in the dark?

from the Japanese of Ise no Tayū

READ THE SIGNS

When I rinsed my spectacles under the tap and wiped them with my
    undershirt,

When every night the striped spider rebuilt her web, triangulating with a
    car aerial that every morning pulled the work apart,

When a man, and then a woman, with orange flags flapping from their
    motorchairs rolled under the kitchen windows, he with one leg, she
    with none,

When the poor streets bore names like *Gold, Paris,* and *Temple,*

When from the Second Baptist Church came a song of dissatisfaction
    with the city of men, in which one tenor predominated, especially
    when he paused to breathe,

When a sign told how at this mission migrants prayed *pardonne-nous nos
    offences,* fed on franks and beans, were handed a few dollars to tide
    them till they disappeared into the mills lit all night,

(mills long shut, town folded for years at dusk),

Here the brightness that caught the eye by the river was only a marble in
    the grass, a wish-fulfilling jewel I put in my pocket,

Here someone mowed grass in circles around a black stone and a white
stone, which married the black stone to the white stone,

Here the Kennebec was too wide fast and deep to swim, though gulls
stood safe on a strange middle shallow,

Here my name inside the rusty box where mail comes, and under that a
bed of Solomon's Seal,

Here the little dirt playground taught with signs the *animals of my
Neighborhood! moose, deer and fawn, coyote, red fox, beaver, fisher,
sea otter, skunk, raccoon, snakes (won't hurt you), ground hog, ospre,
Great Blue heron, STORKS, OWL, squirles, muskrat. We live in the
right place,*

Taught *if you were NOT there, don't use your voice to spread rumors. FINI
– END – Adios – Aloha – hasta la vista, Baby,*

Taught *if you can't make a decision right now, tell the other person you will
get back to them later. Take your time and make the Right Choice. No
Sadness,*

Taught *A Hundred Years Go By Quick* (not knowing then all this would
be gone by spring),

And a Museum of the Streets sign remembered this is the way the
trolley went, how "riding in the wood-sided cars, listening to

the bell clanging, was a pleasure . . . convenient, economical and
pollution-free,"

And a sign taped to that sign said Maggy a longhaired grey aged one
and a half years is missing,

And a window warned "Never Mind the Dog Beware the Owner,"

Where some person entirely without irony let pink petunias overflow
the windowboxes of a white cottage with blue shutters,

Where roses set their autumn hips again, and bittersweet its feral fruit,

Where there was water and the sound of water,

Where a urinous wall inside the former token-booth of the Two-Cent
Bridge (since 1973 on the National Register of Historic Places)
announced *I give Good Head and have a Nice Dick* followed by a
number and *Ask for Travis,*

Where a polished stone explained THIS TREE IS A SYMBOL OF
THE FRIENDSHIP SINCE 1990 BETWEEN KOTLAS,
RUSSIA AND WATERVILLE, MAINE, an idea of Natalia
Kempers who before she passed was "translator of the many
correspondences that arose through the Connection,"

And a man in black, maybe Travis, stepped onto the bridge as I stepped off,

And the tent-moth hid its young in silken bags,

And according to the landlady, Ivan the three-legged cat dodged death
at the shelter by virtue of passionate leanings, wreathings, and
rubbings,

And there was porn for straights but none for gays in the back room
of the local video mart, where a sign requested *please be courteous
and put your choice into the small black bags provided before you bring
it to the counter,*

When work carried me far beyond, Stephen my little wood dove,

When a pickup parked under CAUTION CHANGING RIVER
BOTTOM at the absolute lonesome bottom of an early Sunday
morning boat ramp might have been looking for a sign
of love,
but started his engine and drove away after I gave him my
back for half an hour, didn't turn even once to meet his gaze,

When I washed my door with a rag,
and thought myself the first, the only, the one, the solitary, the
unique.

Then filled the soul with doubt, with every kind of not-knowing,
    and made a song of the cloud of unknowing, which sang

the terrible, deep modesty of creatures, every poor trickling momentary thing

ON THE SURPRISING APPEARANCE OF A STRANGE
PRIEST IN THE AUTHOR'S DREAM DURING A TIME OF
ARDUOUS PRACTICE

asagoto ni

though every morning
the same dust of suffering
must be swept away—
I ask myself
how many lives do you expect,
that you might loiter
through this one?

from an anonymous Japanese poem

ON SEEING THE BLOSSOMS FALL AT A CEREMONY
HONORING THE BUDDHA'S RELICS AT DAIGŌ

kyō mo nao

were I not quite certain

flowers are scattered

for the sake of the Law

today I'd regret them

yet again —

wouldn't I?

from the Japanese of Chinkai Hōshi no Haha

TRANSLATION

at first the 900-year-old scratchings
really seemed to mean,
as I hoped,

it was the same world
after he saved it
as before—

instead,
after further probing,
the poem announced, unhelpfully,

proof he saved the world
is the same
as it has ever been

WRITTEN ON A FOLDED PIECE OF PAPER DURING A SNOWFALL AS THE AUTHOR WAS ABOUT TO ENTER THE PRIESTHOOD

yo no naka ni

my days in the world
    —are vanishing!—

we know about snow:

    falls

    white

    disappears

from the Japanese of Fujiwara Takamitsu

THE SERIES OF MEN MAY BE CONSIDERED AS A SINGLE MAN, LIVING FOREVER, AND CONTINUOUSLY LEARNING

—Pascal

So labor intensive to encode wisdom
                onto DNA,
everybody's already worked so hard,
                spent so much—
wouldn't it be more cost efficient now
                if I were to keep on "donnellying"
forever and continuously? Unless

I got every single thing wrong, and something
                isn't decanting
its ocean of heartbreak juice over and through
                the imbricate seedheads of grasses,
through those thousand waving arms,
                through things on thrones,
breechings at sea, oud music, types and fonts,
                major but mostly minor,
noble but mostly base, bituminous and anthracite
                in the airless dark,
phases, tides, witherings and blunderings
                and burnings-down to the ground,
elements, vessels, organs, circuits, the way fiddles
                finish in scrolls
and old scrolls fox themselves to death,
                fractals, flavors, dryads, trochees,
disgraces and insufficiencies,
                over particles, through waves,

through lists,
       through iambs, through lamb, venison, pork,
through Blake and Kit Smart and Whitman and Ginsberg,
       through secret suffering inward everything.

Unless there's no one to pour and nothing
       everlastingly poured. Then by all means,

what sweet relief for everyone
       to rinse from the slate with a wet sponge
the chalk of my mistake,

       and begin again.

ON LEARNING DEATH IS CLOSE

What we heard was, it started
  with a small numb place

on her leg, but wasn't it just two years ago
  she gave us tea
in the sunroom of her modernist masterpiece
  in the Tuscan foothills?
Since we lifted our cuffs
  shyly away
from the almost-wet luster of her floors?
  Every leaf of hers
shone like jade as we listened
  to plans for the tour
to the East for her husband's work, now
  the luminous children
were grown and situated. *How fit,*
  how beautiful,
we whispered to each other,
  and *how much*
do you imagine this house is worth?

Now we hear it has gone fast
  (lips, limbs,
no movement, no speech),

so what could our own chances be?

Make one exception, the mind begs,
      begin the not-dying with us.

ON THE METAPHOR "THIS BODY IS LIKE A BANANA
TREE"

kaze fukeba

leaves of grass
                    that break at the first gust—

no sooner do I make
                    that likening

than my sleeves
                    are wet with tears

from the Japanese of Former Major Counsellor Kintō

ON THE METAPHOR "THIS BODY IS LIKE THE MOON IN THE WATER"

tsune naranu

to live in the world—
                    I don't expect *that*
                                        to last

because my body
                    is a mortal moon
                                        of water

from the Japanese of Koben

SNAKE HANDLERS

We play this same game
      at the end of every day,
      which you love as much as I:
I have you in a gentle headlock,
      hard against you,
      my mouth, my breath
a graze from your ear—
      but I'm not talking to your ear,
      I'm pouring pictures direct
to your tender brain:
      I will be the Dad,
      You will be the Boy.

I tell you what I'm going to do
      in terms of what has to happen,
      what is inevitable:
Dad's gotta do what Dad's gotta do.
      Things have gone too far
      to turn back now,
I turn every detail
      over like a pebble on my tongue.
      You'll beg for some things to end,
some things to go on forever.
      Some will be the same things.
      Sometimes Dad's rough with his Boy,

might even make his Sonny cry:
> *Dad's gotta do*
> *what Dad's gotta do.*
I hold your hair hard, warn you
> tomorrow you'll ache with emptiness
> and wonder why.
A Boy loves to hide
> *in the crook of Dad's arm,*
> *lives to take care*
of Dad's needs, anytime, anywhere.

The room smells like a stable,
> soft grunting, animals shifting,
> *a Boy's thirsty for anything*
that comes from his Dad: a real Boy
> *can live without food or water for months*
> *on just one look of approval.*
Your eyes half-close, your jaw goes slack—
> bite or not bite,
> it doesn't matter,
the snake can go anywhere now.

IN LOW, UNWORTHY ROOMS HE MADE CARELESS LOVE AND NOW

guesses he's killed some man or men. Can't imagine
how long a pilgrimage could in iron shoes atone.
If all were ignorant, do all bear the blame?

How dared
his indigent seed
lodge a bullet upside anyone's sweet puppy head?

Whose faces? Whose shade
rises, swears *he's the feckless fuckhead who molested my blood.*
His mischief keeps crooning from under the mud

little milk caught the kitty, made off with my heart,
little love in the ditch, little lord that I hurt,
little bug, little bat, broken as dirt

ENGLISH SCENERY

London bombings, 7 July 2005

Instead of spending my day clearing away bits
               of brain and bone,
I washed a cabinet with oil soap and arranged
               blue and white crockery.
Here nothing was on fire. There was no shot from outside,
               I didn't have to pretend
to be dead for hours. No narrow space reflected any blast,
               concentrating its effect,
half a bus did not fly through the air. No "cleanskins" (people
               previously unknown
to the authorities) caused me to be evacuated, or bathed
               my delighted spirit
in fiery floods. No tremor sent each saucer, bowl and jug
               of English scenery
(the way it used to be, or never was) cascading to the floor.
               And no one led me, today,
like a wishfully painted cow, through a lychgate toward
               some distant slaughter.

DAYLIGHT HAS BEEN SAVED BY TIME AGAIN

and now the late April
of the second summer of my fifties is already beginning to burn.
GET UP AND EARN
SOME MONEY is what that light, too much light, says, and also
MILLIONS OF PEOPLE
HAVE BEEN UP FOR HOURS. I know they have, they always have,
every time I keep
an appointment at eight I am astonished at the number of people
already on the road.
You lie lazy and came late to every phase, a voice like my old father's
seems to allege.
"But," I want to argue with the light, "though I came late, I came."
There were years
in the 90s when it looked like I'd rush from spring to winter,
with the rest of my brothers
of the bars and baths and groves of reeds crushed into mazes.
Then I circled back
to have late spring, a real adolescence, even as others were wiping
their mouths of that meal.
Is it greedy then to request late summer, even early autumn?
To ask for a harvest, the wheat
ground so fine you could hold bread to the light and read through it?
Now summer and the work
of that light begin to press down like a kind of war on the earth,
and the real war lowers over us

its magnifying glass, and O my brothers of the bars and baths
             and groves of reeds crushed into mazes,
who ate metal when the wood ought to have been green and then sank
             under the frozen water:
let me rise to work, because there's too much light to sleep.

SENTENCE

By accepting the tight budget of years
left me—
             small yard, narrow bed—
I made peace with the penalty
some say is fixed for those who pour
sexual pleasure over loneliness.

But because a bitter powder
burns my blood sweet every day,
the weird wages of sin in my case
has been life, unprepared-for life,
a stumbling-block for the makers
of sermons because the punishment
we expected never came. Instead

some harsh mercy
(cunning, intricate) emptied
my tomb, prolongs
my days, swells
my account, wreathes
my neck, annoints
my feet, fattens me
on sweetmeats, publishes
my words, magnifies
my bed and husbands it
into outrageous flower.

Fall on me

mountain and hill and rock,
                oh hide me well
from the high-swung
                pendulum of such luck.

MAN KANN NICHT

Unless you hold them hard to your chest
and walk backwards

you will not be able to carry
those many armsful of winter brush

through the narrow gate
to the spring bonfires

NOTES & ACKNOWLEDGMENTS

Thank you to Chase Twichell, Ilya Kaminsky, Eleanor Wilner, Martha Rhodes, James Hoch, Adrian Blevins, Henry Lyman, Kevin Goodan, Kimberly Berwick, Peter Harris, Randall Couch, Robert Thomas and Carol Edelstein for advice on these poems and translations in manuscript. I'm grateful to the Massachusetts Cultural Council for an Artist Fellowship during the time I was completing this book.

Special thanks to Ryan Murphy of Four Way Books, for nudging me toward lyric focus, and to Martha Rhodes, for long kindness.

The epigraph "I give him songs, he gives me length of days" is by Francis Quarles (1592 – 1644), from his *Emblemes*, 1635.

"The Gate to Everywhere": The metaphorical "gate" of the poem is the bodhisattva Avalokiteśvara, called Kannon by the Japanese.

"On the Lungs, the Liver, and the Blood": Togetsukyo Bridge spans the Oi River in Arashiyama, a western district of Kyoto. In the beliefs of the Pure Land sect of East Asian Buddhism, Amida is the Buddha who gathers his devotees after their death into the Western Paradise. The poem is for Larry Schourup and Isao Sano.

"Threat": "like a flame surrounding a flame" (*Ainsi qu'une flamme entoure une flamme*) is from Paul Verlaine's "L'Hiver a cessé."

"Crying the Divine Name in Arabic on Highway 80": The Arabic words *Bismillah* and *Alhumdulillah* mean, respectively, "In the Name of God" and "Praise God."

"Parable of the Conjured City": In Chapter Seven of the Lotus Sutra, the Buddha teaches a parable about a guide who conjures an illusory city as a resting place for discouraged travelers.

"Paradise on Black Ice": The epigraph is from a letter (*Let* 376, 407) Emily Dickinson wrote to her cousins Louisa and Frances. *The Letters of Emily Dickinson*. Thomas H. Johnson and Theodora Ward, eds. 3 vols. Cambridge: Belknap Press of Harvard University Press, 1958.

"Nocturnes of the Brothel of Ruin": The Hebrew letter names of the section titles are in imitation of Couperin's *Leçons de Ténèbres* ("Lessons of Shadows"), a Roman Catholic ceremony for Holy Week, with texts drawn from the Book of Lamentations.

"if there were in the world": The poem alludes to a parable from Chapter Three of the Lotus Sutra, in which a father lures his distracted children out of a burning house (the world of illusion) by promising them three magnificent chariots.

"My Doctor Used to Praise My Ears" is for Michael Donatelli, wherever among the worlds he may be.

"Corpse Flower": The circumstances of Taguchi Shigeyuki's death are recorded in the headnote to one of his poems in the *Kin'yōshū* (645/689). According to Heian-era beliefs, when a death occurred in a house, that house and everyone in it were rendered ritually impure, unable to perform many religious and social functions until a long time had passed. Shigeyuki's hosts may have tried to avoid this inconvenience by carrying him outside the house to die. The poem is for Page Swift Wuerthner.

"Invocation": From ancient times, the Japanese have trained cormorants to catch fish, which are attracted to the surface of the water by the light of small fires hung over the water from boats. Basho wrote a haiku about it: "The cormorant fishing boat/How exciting! But after a while,/I felt sad."

"Oxygen Catastrophe": The title refers to events about 2500 million years ago, when anaerobic organisms that were prevalent on the Earth were poisoned by the large quantities of oxygen produced by other evolving organisms that had developed photosynthesis.

"Homeland" is a variation on "In der Fremde," a poem written in German by Joseph von Eichendorff, and set to music by Robert Schumann in his *Liederkreis*, Op. 39.

Man Kann Nicht: German, "one may not."

I am deeply beholden to Stephen D. Miller for translating the classical Japanese poems with me, and for opening to me the Japan of a thousand years ago and today. The dedication poem, *Kokinshū* 38 by Ki no Tomonori, was read at our wedding:

> my lord   if not to
> you   to whom should I show these
>   blossoms of the plum—
> for you understand the joys
> of their fragrance and splendor

(trans., Laurel Rasplica Rodd, *Kokinshū: A Collection of Poems Ancient and Modern*, Cheng & Tsui Company, 1996, p. 60.)

I regard these versions of Japanese poems as "borrowings," because in a few cases, in incorporating them into my own sequences, I've wandered further from the originals than Stephen and I would contemplate for a scholarly translation. The poems' titles I have adapted (and, in most cases, vigorously pruned) from prose prefaces given the poems centuries ago when they were collected in the Japanese imperial anthologies. The poems' numbering in the anthologies appears after the authors' names below; when there is more than one number, it means there are different versions of the anthology.

The Gate to Everywhere, *yo o sukuu*, Former Major Counsellor Kintō, *Goshūishū* 1196

Sent to the Mountain Temple . . . , *kokoro ni wa*, Jōgon Hōshi, *Kin'yōshū* 629/670

Parable of the Conjured City, *michi toomi*, Mother of Yasusuke no Ō, *Goshūishū* 1193

if there were in the world . . . , *yo no naka ni*, Anonymous, *Shūishū* 1331

the debt/I owe the breasts, *momokusa ni*, Gyōki, *Shūishū* 1347

it hurts/that what I mistook . . . , *tsune yori mo*, Former Preceptor Keisen, *Goshūishū* 1180

To Her Teacher, *kuraki yori*, Izumi Shikibu, *Shūishū* 1342

On the Essence of the *Welling Up Out of the Earth* Chapter, *tarachine wa*, Gon no Sōjō Yōen, *Kin'yōshū* 637/680

I am grateful to the editors of the journals and anthologies in which versions of these poems and translations appeared previously:

American Poetry Review, Asheville Poetry Review, At Length, Barrow Street, The Chattahoochee Review, The Drunken Boat, The Gay & Lesbian Review, Hayden's Ferry Review, Inquiring Mind, Kyoto Journal, The Laurel Review, Literature and Literary Theory, Margie, The Massachusetts Review, Mead, Meridian, Metamorphoses, NOON: The Journal of the Short Poem, Ploughshares, Poetry International, Puerto del Sol, Salamander, Slate Magazine, and *100 American Poets Against the War*

Patrick Donnelly is the author of *The Charge* (Ausable Press, 2003; since 2009 part of Copper Canyon Press), and co-translator with Stephen D. Miller of the Japanese poems in *The Wind from Vulture Peak: The Buddhification of Japanese Waka in the Heian Period*. He is an associate editor of *Poetry International*, director of the Advanced Seminar at The Frost Place, and has taught writing at the Lesley University MFA Program, Colby College, the Bread Loaf Writers' Conference, and elsewhere. He is a recipient of an Artist Fellowship from the Massachusetts Cultural Council. His poems have appeared in many journals, including *American Poetry Review*, *The Massachusetts Review*, *Ploughshares*, *The Virginia Quarterly Review*, and *The Yale Review*, and have been anthologized in *The Book of Irish American Poetry from the 18th Century to the Present*.

Stephen D. Miller is assistant professor of Japanese language and literature at the University of Massachusetts, Amherst. Miller is author of *The Wind from Vulture Peak: The Buddhification of Japanese Waka in the Heian Period*, a scholarly history and analysis forthcoming from Cornell East Asia Series. He is translator of *A Pilgrim's Guide to Forty-Six Temples* (Weatherhill Inc., 1990) and editor of *Partings at Dawn: An Anthology of Japanese Gay Literature* (Gay Sunshine Press, 1996). He lived in Japan for nine years between 1980 and 1999, in part as the recipient of two Japan Foundation fellowships for research abroad.

Donnelly and Miller's translations have appeared or are forthcoming in *Bateau*, *Cha: An Asian Literary Journal*, *Circumference*, *The Drunken Boat*, *eXchanges*, *Inquiring Mind*, *Kyoto Journal*, *Mead*, *Metamorphoses*, *New Plains Review*, *NOON: The Journal of the Short Poem*, *Poetry International*, and *Like Clouds or Mists: Studies and Translations of Nō Plays of the Genpei War*. Donnelly and Miller are married and live in Western Massachusetts.